IMAGES
of America

NISQUALLY
INDIAN TRIBE

ON THE COVER: Indian labor helped build Washington. Here several Nisqually families in the Puyallup Valley wait to have their picture taken alongside Indian hops pickers from other parts of the country. Hops harvested in the Puyallup Valley were exported to flavor European beers. This late-1800s photograph includes traditional Indian women identified by their distinctive head scarves and shawls. A male relative of Antoine Jackson (Nisqually, at center) holds a child in his lap. Another woman wears a decorated spruce root hat, a gift she received or perhaps a craft item she hopes to sell after the hops season. The Pincus farm hired Nisquallies, and the Wren farm was dependent on Indian labor from Canada and areas east of the mountains. (Courtesy Cecelia Svinth Carpenter.)

IMAGES
of America

NISQUALLY
INDIAN TRIBE

Cecelia Svinth Carpenter, Maria Victoria Pascualy,
and Trisha Hunter

ARCADIA
PUBLISHING

Published by Arcadia Publishing
Charleston, South Carolina

Library of Congress Catalog Card Number: 2007935829

For all general information contact Arcadia Publishing at:
Telephone 843-853-2070
Fax 843-853-0044
E-mail sales@arcadiapublishing.com
For customer service and orders:
Toll-Free 1-888-313-2665

Visit us on the Internet at www.arcadiapublishing.com

This book is dedicated with love and affection to our mothers,
Mary Edna Binder Svinth and Ofelia Olaya de Pascualy.

CONTENTS

ACKNOWLEDGMENTS

We want to thank the Nisqually tribe today as well as all the Nisqually who walked before us and regrettably go unnamed in this book. The struggles of many individuals ensured the survival of the tribe and made this book possible. Special thanks to Jack Curtright, Cynthia Iyall, Georgianna Kautz, Bud McBride, Zelma McCloud, Elaine Miller, Richard Schneider, Lou Ann Squally, and the archives of the Washington State Historical Society, which each day contributes more and more to the story of Indian people in our state. All photographs in this work have come from the private collection of Cecelia Svinth Carpenter unless otherwise credited.

INTRODUCTION

The traditional lands of the Nisqually reached north to join the lands of the Puyallups, with whom we shared "in-common lands" in and about the present towns of Parkland and Spanaway. To the south, we claimed the present towns of Rainier and Tenino to meet the lands of the Cowlitz and the Chehalis. On the northwest, our lands bordered on the Puget Sound, the Whulge as we called it, and extended into the islands therein. To the east, our boundaries extended to the topmost point on Mount Rainier, or Tacobet as we called the mountain. We had at least 13 permanent villages, which were located where the smaller, smoother waters of the tributaries entered the Nisqually River. There was also a village on McAllister Creek, one at Sequalitchew Creek, one at the south end of Nisqually Lake, and another near Roy. The villages at South Bay and Olympia were located in our traditional land-use area and, although they had their own identity, at the time of the treaty, the occupants of these villages came onto our reservation. We call them "associated villages" because so many of our people had married into those villages.

Our name in traditional times was Squalli or Squalli-absch, meaning the people of the Squalli. We had bestowed the name Squalli onto the prairie grass on the vast prairies that lay on both sides of our river in those days. The river took its name from the prairie grass. We took our name from the prairie grass and the river. We called ourselves the Squalli-absch, the People of the Grass Country, the People of the River.

The Nisqually River flowed through the heart of our land and was the lifeblood of our people. This river not only provided a home for the salmon, our main source of food supply, but also provided fresh water as well as a highway down through the center of our land connecting most of our villages into a workable unit.

The British came in 1833 to establish a fur-collecting fort at the mouth of Sequalitchew Creek, just about a half-mile east of the Nisqually River delta. These new people represented the Hudson's Bay Company. The employees there were mostly single men who married women from our villages. We had little problem with the British. They would be leaving soon, or so we thought. That did not happen. Instead we were to learn that the British and the Americans had an agreement of joint occupation concerning this land area that they called the Oregon Country. In 1846, these two nations set their dividing boundary at the 49th degree north latitude, which placed our lands and our people under the jurisdiction of the United States.

Fort Steilacoom, an American military fort, was set up five miles to the east of us on the Steilacoom River in 1848. About the same time, the American settlers began to pour into Squalli country, arriving with their American wives and children and requesting land to farm under the Donation Land Act. Had we fought the foreigners off at the beginning, we might have succeeded.

When Isaac I. Stevens was sent here to become the first territorial governor, he set about negotiating treaties with the various tribes. He desired to extinguish our claim to our land while allowing us to reserve some of our land for our homes. The Medicine Creek Treaty was the first treaty to be made. It included our tribe, our Puyallup neighbors, and the Indian people at the lower end of the Whulge. Three reservations were to be established. Leschi and Quaymuth were to sign for us, but, upon learning that our reserve was to be on the high-forested land to the west of the delta, Leschi refused to sign. He wanted our reserved lands to be located on the river where our people could fish.

Well, we would not move onto our reserved lands. Believing Leschi and Quaymuth to be troublemakers, those in charge at Olympia decided to send militia, mounted rangers, out to our river to take the two into custody, protective custody, that is. Word spread fast, and by the time the Eaton Rangers, a volunteer militia, had come out from Olympia to pick up our leaders, they had fled with their families into the hills. They, and other warriors and their families, crossed the Puyallup River where Puyallup warriors joined them. The entire group stopped at the White River and stood their ground. The time was October. The year was 1855. The Treaty War of 1855–1856 had begun.

The war lasted about nine months. It was a sad war with casualties on both sides. Indian agents ordered the men, women, and children who didn't go into the battle area in the mountain foothills to internment camps on Fox Island and Squaxon Island. Many of us died in the squalid camp conditions. The end of the war came when Stevens agreed to change the locations of both the Nisqually and the Puyallup reserves to good lands on our respective rivers. Stevens requested the Indian leaders to come in and give themselves up. The Indian warriors had been defeated in the war and reluctantly returned to the area. Quaymuth turned himself in and was murdered as he slept in the governor's office that first night. Leschi returned from east of the mountains where he had fled and was eventually taken into custody. Someone had to take the blame for the war, and Leschi became the scapegoat. He was arrested and tried in the territorial court on the charge that he had killed one man—A. Benton Moses.

The professional army from Fort Steilacoom had participated in the war but those in command there felt it was wrong to accuse and try a soldier, Leschi, as a civilian. The soldiers showed their disapproval, first by attempting to prove Leschi innocent of the charges brought against him and second by refusing to let the hangman's gallows be built on the property of Fort Steilacoom. The gallows were constructed on the prairie over by Lake Steilacoom, and on February 19, 1858, Leschi, last chief of the Nisqually people, was hung.

What Leschi requested did come about. He wanted a better location for the Nisqually Reservation. He wanted a place for our people to fish, a place to graze our horses. This was granted. For this, he paid the supreme price. If we had not kept our reserved lands, we would have disappeared, I suppose. Some of our women had married British and American men, and those ladies went with their husbands onto donation land claims of either 320 or 640 acres. Our men did not qualify for this type of land because one had to be a United States citizen to sign up for land and, you guessed it, we weren't citizens! Not until 1924, to be exact, were all of us considered citizens. Some of our people who had received allotments in the 1880s became citizens, but most of us did not.

When we believed that things could get no worse, word came that the portion of our reservation that lay on the Pierce County side of the Nisqually River was to be condemned for a military base. Our condemnation map of 1918–1920 shows that most of our living took place on that side of the river. There were at least 13 homes, 6 cemeteries, 2 churches, and the tribal headquarters—all of which represented probably three-fourths of our people, who were now to be displaced. There was only one thing to do, and that was to move our people across the river to the remainder of our reservation. The problem there was that that portion of our reservation had also been divided and allotted into family units, so only those families who were heirs or were related to these landowners could establish themselves there.

Because of this problem, the government gave us a chance to select "in-lieu" lands, or in-place-of lands to explain the term, which could be purchased with the money coming from the sale price of the condemned lands. These in-lieu lands would be placed under a tax-free status such as the reservation lands were under. Like many families who had no relatives on the Thurston County side of the river, my family selected in-lieu lands, but the government refused to approve the sale by proclaiming that the price of the new land was too high to make the exchange. Thus, my family became part of a new group who had to select land farther away from the reservation. Our group became known as the dispossessed Nisquallies.

In 1932, Pete Kalama made a list of 210 "breeds," those of part-Indian blood, to be added to the tribal membership rolls. My mother's name was on that list. My name was on that list. The tribal council accepted those people on that list as tribal members. They needed more people. This list represented those who had not received land allotments because they had been born during the generation following the assignments of the allotments. Many on the list were descendants of those who had lost their land in the 1918 condemnation. After the list had been accepted by the tribal council, it was sent to the Bureau of Indian Affairs for approval. The BIA sent the list back unapproved.

In 1933, Congress passed the Indian Reorganization Act. It stated that if Indian tribes would write tribal constitutions and reorganize their tribal government, federal money could be funneled into our community. We wrote a tribal constitution, which was accepted in 1945. I attended those meetings with my mother. Enrollment now became the vehicle through which our people were to become "legal" voting tribal members. Our constitution provided requirements for this enrollment. A special committee drew up a list of members. The number of voting adults added up to only 61 people. Many were left off of this list. Many had moved to and were living on other reservations or were lost in white towns and cities. After the membership list appeared, the infighting began to separate family members and pitted brother against brother. The pain I saw in some of those who were left off of the list plagued me greatly. The 1945 roll remained. It was opened once in 1963, just briefly. It was not opened again until 1974, when the Boldt Fishing Decision mandated that all tribes who were parties of the case must open their rolls to all of those who met the enrollment requirements.

Our five-member tribal council was elected every two years. We became absorbed in researching and giving testimonies. In the 1940s, the Indian Land Claims Commission was established in Washington, D.C., to address the fact that many tribes had not been paid for lands ceded in the treaties. During the 1950s and 1960s, there seemed to be an increase in the commercial fishing industry. The non-Indian fishermen began to complain that the Indian fishermen who were fishing in their usual and accustomed places as per the treaty should fish only on the waters within the boundaries of their reservations. Many minor wars broke out on the riverbanks of both the Nisqually and the Puyallup Rivers between the Indian fishermen and non-Indian fishermen. Finally, the decision as to where our Indian fishermen could or could not fish was taken to federal court. After a lengthy court battle, the Boldt Decision was issued in 1974 proclaiming our right to fish in our old "usual and accustomed" fishing stations "in common with the citizens of the territory." The Boldt Decision also instructed the tribal councils to open their enrollment rolls and enroll all eligible Indian people as per tribal constitution requirements.

I applied for enrollment here at Nisqually, my mother's tribe, and I was enrolled in the fall of 1974. I served as tribal vice-chairman during the 1975–1976 administration. Our council, called the Business Council, was made up of five tribal members who carried out the wishes of the General Council, who, according to our tribal constitution, held the ultimate power of decision-making. During those two years, I observed many things taking place. Our membership enrollment was increasing, and our people were returning to become enrolled. Our headquarters for the day-to-day business of the tribe was in a rented building in Yelm because there were no buildings on the reservation large enough to house our operation. We first rented rooms in the old Methodist church in Yelm, then we moved out east of town into an old motel building. By this time, we now had a tribal police force made up of two officers whose job it was to patrol the river and our fishermen.

During the final months of the 1975–1976 administration, our treasurer, George Kalama, along with our chairman, Zelma McCloud, and our business manager made an application for funds to the federal government to build a fish-net facility. The plans included not only a huge gymnasium-type space for the enterprise but also additional space for tribal offices. As we left office, we learned that the application had been approved. Land adjacent to the remaining reservation was purchased for the facility, and in 1977, ground was broken. In 1978, the new building was dedicated. The main building housed the council chambers, the accounting department, the planning department, the education department, the social services department, and the fisheries or natural resources department. We later added a senior citizen–head start building, which also houses our medical and dental services. As we slowly brought our people back to become enrolled, to live in the new housing and urban development homes built on the reservation, life returned to our land.

Today we have restored 1,200 acres to our land base through purchase. The Indian culture wraps itself around each one of us and binds us together as a family unit, just like the extended family of old. Our ancestors were dependent entirely on the natural world and on each other. The people, the land, and the water were spiritually bonded together as one. That bonding process is still a built-in part of us, and although time has tossed us about, the grinding and crushing has not pulverized us but has polished us, and through the years, we have become stronger. Despite the battles, we are still here.

—Cecelia Svinth Carpenter

One

PEOPLE OF THE
SQUALLY RIVER

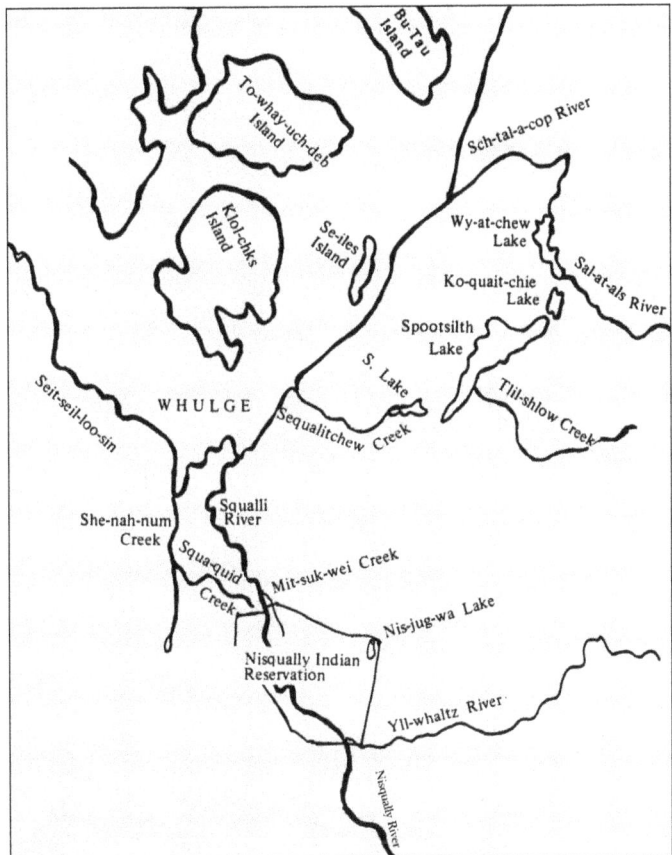

Cecelia Carpenter's map shows Nisqually place names on the Whulge. The Whulge, or Salish Sea, encompasses waters from the Strait of Georgia, north of the Fraser River, to the southern edge of Puget Sound. The Whulge also encompasses the Nisqually watershed. In traditional times, village identity was tied to the watersheds, and people often took their name from waters close to home. Rivers and streams were also home to the salmon that provided the Nisqually with physical, cultural, and spiritual sustenance.

The Nisqually people (people of the Squally River) lived in 13 villages located along freshwater streams and saltwater beaches. A series of prairies or plains led to Tacobet (Mount Rainier), the spiritual center of the people. The cities and towns of Olympia, Dupont, Yelm, Roy, and Elbe stand on the site of Nisqually villages. As seen here in 1906, Tacobet nestles in its bosom the Indian reservation school that served South Sound Indian children. The Medicine Creek Treaty, the first treaty signed in Washington, transferred most of this Indian land to the U.S. government. (Courtesy University of Washington Libraries.)

Eighty-some miles of river flow through the traditional homelands of the Nisqually people, including Nisqually Canyon, pictured here in 1910. The river flows from a glacier high on Tacobet (Mount Rainier), and then travels across the foothills, on through heavily wooded areas, then streams down through the meadows and prairies to empty into the Whulge. Nisqually lived mostly in the lower sections of the river and fished in the middle sections. Homes were not built in the thick wooded cover that adorned the middle section. Villages appeared one after another on the lower banks of the Nisqually River. (Courtesy University of Washington Libraries.)

Mary Edna (Nisqually) was born in 1887 when being Indian was not something one had to prove. Indian people document their ethnicity because of the legal obligation the federal government has with descendants of signatories to treaties. Some government agencies require a blood quantum of one-fourth Indian blood. Tribes themselves also set criteria for enrollment of a tribal member. Skin color is a poor marker of Indian-ness.

TAHOMA RESEARCH SERVICE Fort
9609 SOUTH SHERIDAN AVE. Nisqually
TACOMA, WA 93444
" Indian Lodge of Lach-ah-lett "
by Paul Kane 1846-48

Artist Paul Kane sketched *Indian Lodge of Lach-ah-Lett* in 1846. Lach-ah-Lett was one of the first Nisqually to be written about by outsiders. Nisqually culture was oral so it is not known what Indians thought of the outsiders who so willingly left behind loved ones and homelands. In 1909, the Dupont Powder Works Company was built on top of Lach-ah-Lett's village site. Today the powder works is gone and in its place is the town of DuPont. (Courtesy Royal Ontario Museum.)

13

American forts (like Fort Steilacoom pictured here) were built to protect American civilians from Indians yet were often given the name of the tribe on whose land they squatted. Indian place names documented important events from the time of creation, the names of families associated with the land, or foodstuffs that could be harvested in the area. Indian place names were encoded with cultural history. Tacobet, the spiritual center of the Nisqually, rises at a distance from Fort Steilacoom. (Courtesy Oregon Historical Society.)

Londoner Edward Huggins's letters, and newspaper articles, provide snapshots of early Nisqually Indian interaction with the British and the Americans before and after the 1854 treaty. Huggins knew Chief Leschi, who became the most important leader of the Nisqually. Edward Huggins married Letitia Work, the mixed-blood daughter of Hudson's Bay Company trader John Work, in 1857 after the Treaty Wars.

William Tolmie and Edward Huggins were employed by Hudson's Bay Company, a British fur-gathering corporation. Tolmie was 21 when he first came to Indian country. He married Jane, one of the mixed-blood daughters of Hudson's Bay Company trader John Work. Tolmie's youngest son, Simon Fraser Tolmie, became premier of Canada in 1928. Tolmie's journal provides glimpses of early Nisqually Indian life. Tolmie, along with other whites, actively tried to prevent Chief Leschi's hanging after the Treaty Wars.

Hudson's Bay Company employees were encouraged to marry Indian women, as it was good for trade. Charley Ross Jr., who stands to the left in traditional Scottish attire, had an Indian mother and a Scottish father. He in turn worked for the food-growing arm of the Hudson's Bay Company, the Puget Sound Agricultural Company, and married a Nisqually woman, Catherine Tumalt Ross. In this photograph, probably taken around 1870, she holds their child in her lap.

15

The Ross farm, pictured here around 1900, as well as Nisqually Lake, is now part of the Fort Lewis Military Base, which absorbed two-thirds of Nisqually Reservation lands.

Catherine Tumalt Ross (born 1834) lived with her husband, Charley Ross Jr., on a farm close to Nisqually Lake. She shows her status through the combed back hair and formal corseted outfit. Within early South Sound society, race and class were expressed through social markers like clothes and hairstyles.

Catherine Tumalt Ross (Nisqually, at right) travels with her daughter Mary in a horse-drawn buggy around 1910. Mary was born in 1853, a year before the Medicine Creek Treaty was negotiated between the South Sound tribes and the U.S. government. After the treaty, some Indian people settled on reservation lands while others continued living in mixed society.

Nisqually Prairie, around 1920, was one of the vast open prairies encompassed within present-day Pierce County. Prairies or plains were used by Nisqually to graze horses as well as harvest camas and other wild foods that formed an essential part of the Indian larder. The transfer of most of the Nisqually prairie land to the United States signifies an unacknowledged transfer of wealth from one nation to another. (Courtesy University of Washington Libraries.)

Indian architecture included a variety of forms. Massive cedar-plank houses built at the site of permanent villages were considered inheritable property. Photographed in 1900, this temporary shelter is of a type quickly constructed during hunting trips or temporary movements and later abandoned.

The Nisqually sweat lodge, as seen here, was made of a framework of switches covered by twigs and brush and then compacted with earth. A depression on the floor provided a place for hot stones, which were heated by a fire built outside of the lodge. Blankets or mats covered the door. Hot stones were heated and rolled into the lodge pit where they were sprinkled with water to create steam. Both Nisqually men and women used steam for purification and medicinal purposes. Sweats, however, were detrimental when used against diseases carried in by outsiders, such as measles. Estimates suggest half the indigenous population of Puget Sound died from disease before 1840.

18

The Sales cabin, pictured in 1910, was built on Nisqually Prairie, or present-day Parkland, Washington, in the mid-1850s. The homes of the early settlers only sheltered one family and were small in contrast to the plank houses of the Nisqually, which housed several families. Indian society was based on the communal use of land and resources while settler society idealized individual achievement and personal property.

Visitors can see a re-created South Sound cedar-plank home at the Washington State History Museum in Tacoma. No original homes survive as many were burned down by outsiders or left behind by displaced villagers. Fran and Bill James (Lummi) wove the wall mats that helped keep the house warm. Karen Reed (Puyallup) constructed the clam basket, and Lance Wilkie (Makah) hand adzed the planks and constructed the home using traditional techniques. Author Maria Pascualy was chief curator of the permanent exhibit, but the content of the Indian story was developed with the guidance of many Indian people. Author Cecelia Carpenter was the lead consultant on the plank house.

Some Nisqually women wore cedar bark skirts and fur or cedar capes to keep warm in cold weather. The shredded cedar was soft to the touch and also helped water drip off quickly if it rained. Well-to-do Nisqually tended to favor buckskin garb. Western-style clothes were adopted for a variety of reasons. Military caps and jackets were status-laden regalia much coveted by Indian men in the earliest period. The use of store-bought clothes was also convenient as they were easier to acquire than those made by weaving cedar or working skins. This staged image by photographer Edward Curtis was taken in 1912 in Puget Sound.

NISQUALLY MISSION HOUSE

The Methodist Church sent missionaries to Nisqually country in 1839, but a lack of interest among the local Indian people meant the enterprise was abandoned after two years. The Methodist Mission, which was built close to the traditional burial grounds of the local people, was burnt down once the missionaries left. This rough sketch taken from a newspaper account shows the mission in 1839.

Nisqually had reservation land in what are now Pierce County and Thurston County. This map shows the size of the Pierce County section of the reservation, which was condemned and developed into Fort Lewis.

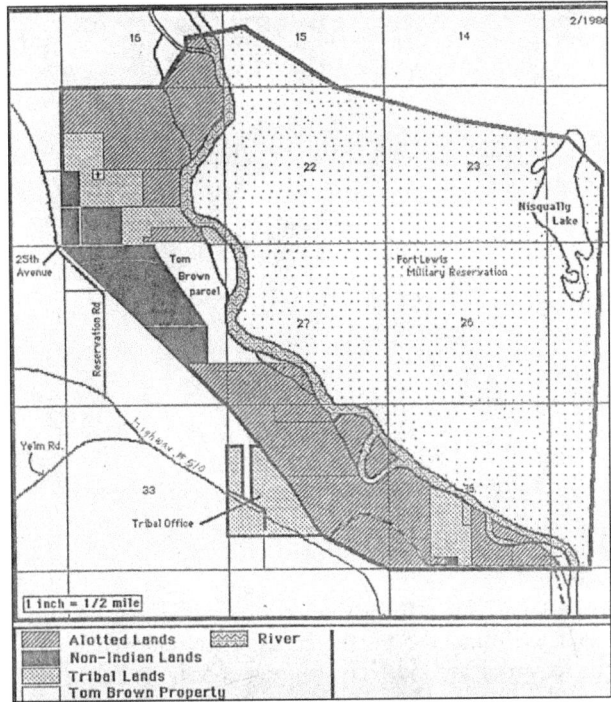

Outsiders who settled in the Northwest encountered unfamiliar terrain and were often dependent on the expertise and generosity of the Indian people. These two settlers, around 1890, are spear fishing, probably imitating the techniques of Indian fishers who could often harvest fish without nets. Fish runs were once spectacularly so abundant that white farmers used salmon to fertilize their fields. This was contrary to Nisqually notions of food use and respect for the salmon.

Traditional Indian fishing practices insured that salmon would thrive and return. Fish traps, or weirs, were quickly constructed and then removed as needed to allow the salmon to continue to the spawning grounds. This photograph shows Yelm Jim's house and fish trap on a creek flowing into the Puyallup River on the reservation. Yelm Jim looks at the photographer from the edge of the bank (second from the left). Different families had rights to certain fisheries but usually allowed others to also use them if asked. Problems arose when food-gathering areas were used without permission.

Nisqually who lived near the saltwater buried their dead in trees; those inland buried the dead in the ground. White towns and cities edged out the Nisqually, and tribal burial grounds were soon cleared for sale. Disturbed grave goods were sometimes taken as souvenirs or were donated to museums. This c. 1910 picture was probably taken during a clearing.

When Nisqually practiced ground burial, the body was placed in a sitting position as seen in this photograph. Some bodies were wrapped in cedar bark blankets, head pointing west, with the soil mounded up and marked with hand-sized rocks. Burials of this type can still be found at Fort Lewis, which was once Nisqually land. Historian Edmond Meany (born 1862) took this unidentified image. (Courtesy University of Washington Libraries.)

Many Nisqually people are still part of the Shaker Church. Shakers followed an oral religion that was revealed to John Slocum, a Squaxin, in 1882. Shaker teachings blend Indian traditions and Christian beliefs. Shaker services can be identified by handbells, as seen on the table, or by the gesture of an uplifted open palm.

The late

General Isaac I. Stevens

Killed in the battle of Chantilly
September 1st 1862.

This lithograph memorializes the death of territorial governor Isaac Stevens during the Civil War. Stevens considered the Medicine Creek Treaty, signed with the Nisqually and other South Sound tribes, a trial run for all the other treaties he planned to negotiate. In preparation for the treaty, he instructed settler Michael Simmons to designate friendly Indians as chiefs. Quaymuth, Leschi, and their brother-in-law Stahi were designated chiefs and subchiefs. Isaac Stevens expected his appointees to sign the treaty.

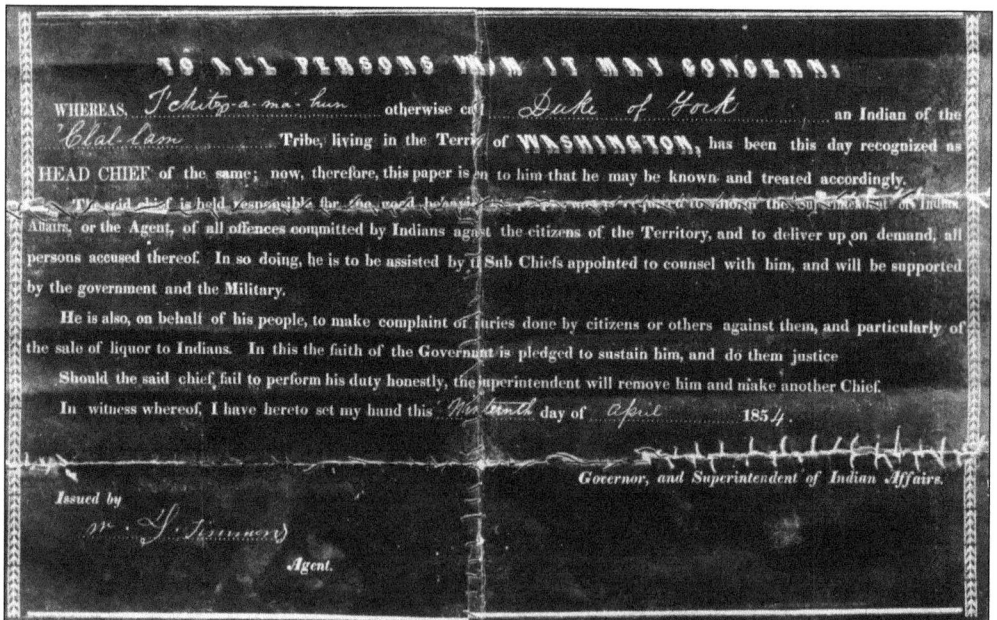

TO ALL PERSONS WHOM IT MAY CONCERN:

WHEREAS, T'chitop-a-ma-hun otherwise call Duke of York an Indian of the 'Clal-lam Tribe, living in the Terr' of **WASHINGTON**, has been this day recognized as HEAD CHIEF of the same; now, therefore, this paper is en to him that he may be known and treated accordingly.

The said chief is held responsible for the good behavior .... the Superintendent of Indian Affairs, or the Agent, of all offences committed by Indians against the citizens of the Territory, and to deliver up on demand, all persons accused thereof. In so doing, he is to be assisted by the Sub Chiefs appointed to counsel with him, and will be supported by the government and the Military.

He is also, on behalf of his people, to make complaint of injuries done by citizens or others against them, and particularly of the sale of liquor to Indians. In this the faith of the Government is pledged to sustain him, and do them justice

Should the said chief fail to perform his duty honestly, the superintendent will remove him and make another Chief.

In witness whereof, I have hereto set my hand this Nineteenth day of April 1854.

Governor, and Superintendent of Indian Affairs.

Issued by
Mr. J. Simmons
Agent.

As part of the treaty-making process, territorial governor Isaac Stevens, contrary to Indian custom, said men he chose and made chiefs with a certificate, like this one, would speak for all the people. This certificate belonged to Pat Kanim, a northern Indian who was a traditional enemy of the Nisqually and later worked as a scout for the Americans during the Treaty Wars. (Courtesy University of Washington Libraries, Special Collections.)

This portrait of Quaymuth, Leschi's brother, was drawn for a newspaper article after treaty times. Copies of the image were sold as souvenirs. Indian people lost a generation of leaders after the treaty. Quaymuth was murdered in Gov. Isaac Stevens's office after surrendering during the Indian wars; Leschi was hung; Owhi, Leschi's Yakama cousin, was shot; Qualchan, Owhi's son, was hung; Walla Walla head chief Peo Peo Mox Mox (Yellow Bird) was shot and skinned by Oregon militia; and Cowlitz leader Umtux was hung at the close of the war.

Nisqually Indian Brother of Leschi.

Quiemulth

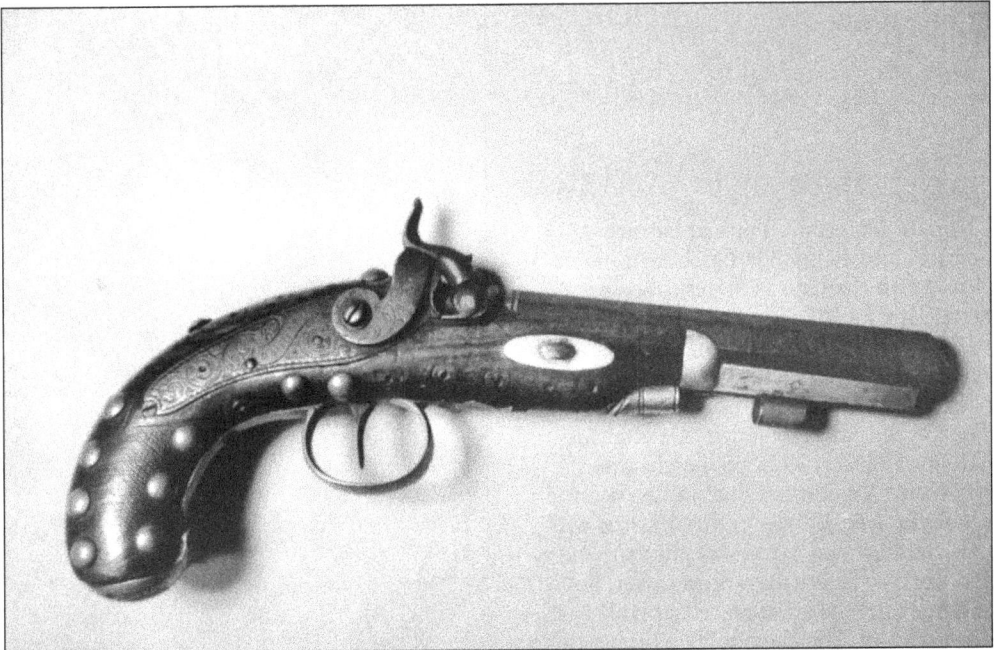

The Treaty Wars lasted nine months after the South Sound tribes were assigned rocky lands away from their rivers. Leschi was reluctant to turn himself in as many of his relatives had been killed. Once Leschi knew he was going to be apprehended, either he gave his pistol to or had it taken by Tyee Dick.

Tyee Dick (E-la-kah-ka) was a treaty signer and a combatant in the Treaty Wars, in which the South Sound tribes fought for better lands. After the Americans apprehended Leschi, some accounts suggest Tyee Dick became headman of the Puyallup and Nisqually. Today Tyee Dick has many descendants among the Nisqually, Puyallup, and Cowlitz people. (Courtesy McBride-Schneider.)

The most important figure in Nisqually political history is Chief Leschi, who went to war with the United States to secure better land for his people. After the Treaty Wars, Leschi was charged with murder for his wartime activities and became the first person executed in Washington territory. This portrait was probably made after his hanging February 19, 1858. Leschi was considered a modern Indian in his day, and he is portrayed as such in this drawing with hair cut short and a store-bought shirt. Most accounts say he usually wore a jacket, but in this drawing, the artist placed a blanket on his shoulders. The diagonal line on his cheek may be the scar that was used to identify him by one or two witnesses during his trial. In 2004, the Nisqually tribe succeeding in having Leschi exonerated.

Chief Leschi

Leschi's purported mark is the first on the top right of the last page of the Medicine Creek Treaty, signed in 1854. Leschi said he did not sign the treaty. Indian people did not have a written language, so one of Isaac Stevens's men wrote each leader's name and then the tribal representative would make his mark or "X" next to his name. Leschi and his people say he refused to sign because Stevens denied his people the original river lands and prairies they requested. (Courtesy National Archives.)

Ralph Chaplin, Wobbly hero, poet, and resident of Tacoma, Washington, wrote a poem in 1960 in honor of Leschi called "Only the Drums Remembered." Leschi's portrait, also drawn by Chaplin, includes the star the Nisqually say rose in the sky when Leschi was born. The distinctive hairstyle is described as one used by South Sound warriors in battle. (Courtesy Washington State Historical Society.)

LESCHI

CAMP ON THE TREATY GROUND.

James Swan's drawing of the Chehalis Treaty grounds suggests how the Medicine Creek Treaty encampment may have looked. Men, women, and children attended the treaty council, which lasted three days in late December 1854. Hazard, Isaac Stevens's son, signed the treaty as a 13-year-old and described the treaty council at length in his father's biography.

Chief Wallihee, 1911, was a Klickitat from Leschi's mother's tribe, and like Leschi, he farmed a little, sold game to outsiders, and continued to gather traditional foods throughout his life. The U.S. government actively promoted farming after the treaty, although the big profits were made in real estate. Several American treaty signers had already invested in land before the treaty was signed. (Courtesy Oregon Historical Society.)

Pictured here around 1880, Ezra Meeker, author of an early history of Chief Leschi, poses in leathers, as did many pioneers and tourists who were apparently charmed by Indian garb once Indian lands were transferred to the United States. The transcript of Leschi's first trial was destroyed by fire, so Meeker's firsthand account of events is often used by historians.

Leschi awaited his execution at the guardhouse at Fort Steilacoom after the Treaty Wars. Military men like Lt. Augustus Kautz, married to Leschi's niece Kitty Kautz, tried unsuccessfully to get Leschi a fair trail. Many settlers also disagreed with hanging a military combatant during a time of war. Leschi was the first person in the Washington Territory to be legally executed.

Benjamin Franklin Shaw was interpreter at the Medicine Creek Treaty Council and later served in the volunteer militia during the Treaty Wars. In 1856, Shaw led the militia in a massacre of 60 Indian women and children in Oregon that went unpunished. In 1905, he wrote, "If Leschi had been provided with provisions and ammunition, with a few more men like himself, he would have put up a stiff fight for us in the dense woods." Shaw, in his old age, poses in his Indian leathers in an undated photograph. (Courtesy Washington State Historical Society.)

American soldiers reluctantly kept Leschi at the guardhouse in Steilacoom. Alliances were clouded in the South Sound during the war—Charles Eaton, part of the militia that imprisoned Leschi, was married to the chief's daughter Kalakala. Did he try to help his wife's relative? Nisqually did not have a written language, and there are no records from their point of view of what happened. (Courtesy Oregon Historical Society.)

Kitty Kautz was Leschi's niece, and she married an American military man named Augustus Kautz. An artist's interpretation from a c. 1900 newspaper article is the only image of her. Kautz's descendants still live and work on the Nisqually Reservation.

Gus Kautz was the son of Augustus Kautz, an American army officer, and Kitty Kautz, Leschi's niece. Gus's brother, Neugen Kautz, educated at Chemawa Indian School, represented his people in legal matters and was involved in the transfer of Indian lands during the allotment period. The allotment act of 1887 took lands held communally by Indian people and turned them into personal property that could be bought and sold.

Fort Steilacoom, established in 1849, was the first army post on Puget Sound. It was built on Chambers Creek in reaction to settler fears after the Whitman killings in Walla Walla. Many of the Steilacoom people who lived here joined the Nisqually. Western State Hospital is now located here. (Courtesy Oregon Historical Society.)

Diaked, a treaty signer, was killed during the Treaty Wars. Ha-pa-ce-wud, now elderly, was his wife. Her clothes are made from store-bought cloth, but her basketry hat (on the floor) is traditional. The killer was Pat Kanim, a Snoqualmie Indian who worked for territorial governor Isaac Stevens as a scout. Stevens paid well for Nisqually heads. Other tribes like the Cowlitz also sided with the Americans. Alliances were not clear-cut in territorial days.

Wahoolit, or Yelm Jim, fought with Leschi during the Treaty Wars. Jim was said to have thunder power, which saved him from hanging after the war. He avenged Leschi's betrayal to the American militia by shooting Sluggia. (Sluggia is often described as Leschi's nephew, but there is no genealogical evidence to support this). The photographer probably placed the skull in the image as a symbol of the murder as well as to sell more pictures. A Salish blanket hangs behind Yelm Jim.

This contemporary (1974) interpretation of a pioneer map of Thurston County shows the land as a resource to be evaluated according to the market value of trees that can be logged or land that can be cultivated. This point of view did not make sense to Indian people, who held land communally and derived their identity and history from it. (Courtesy Washington State Historical Society.)

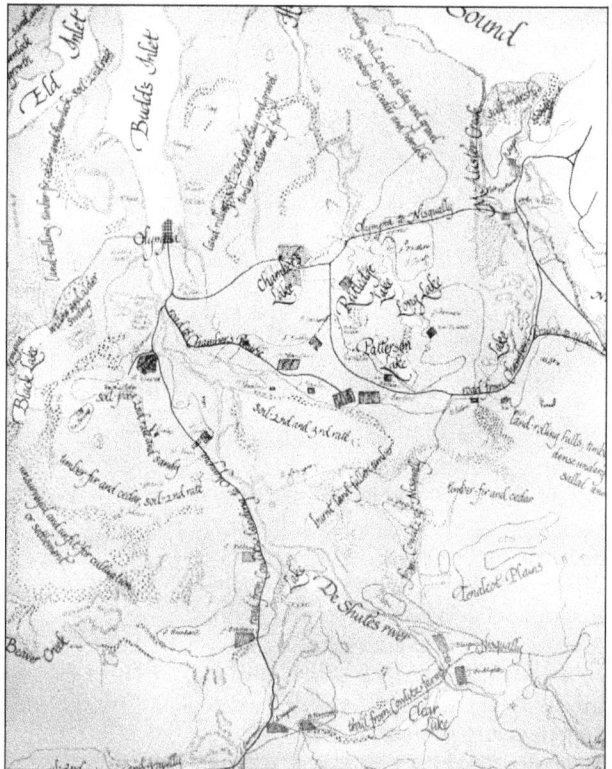

A group of history buffs tour Camp Montgomery, a log structure located in present-day Spanaway around 1900. Hudson's Bay Company employees living on Muck Creek were considered a threat because their Indian wives might pass on information to Leschi's men during the Treaty Wars. Isaac Stevens ordered the Muck Creek men to leave their homes and relocate to Camp Montgomery where they could be watched. The Muck Creek men refused and were imprisoned. (Courtesy Washington State Historical Society.)

Here the Medicine Creek treaty tree (second from the left) stands tall, before Interstate 5 cut through the treaty grounds in the 1960s. The treaty tree is a symbol of Leschi and treaty rights to the Nisqually people. Originally, a grove of firs marked the treaty council grounds, but eventually one tree was recognized as the final witness to the signing of the treaty. In 2006, after the exoneration of Chief Leschi, a storm knocked down the remaining snag. The tree is now safely stored on the reservation.

George P. Bonney, curator of the Ferry Museum, erected a marker in 1922 showing the spot where the Medicine Creek Treaty was negotiated. The treaty site was later bisected by Interstate 5 and covered by a gas station. The marker is pictured at its present site on page 120. (Courtesy Washington State Historical Society.)

Chief Leschi and Quaymuth were reburied together on July 4, 1895. Bill Quaymuth (left), Luke, George Leschi, Yelm Jim, and Old Steilacoom (far right) handled the reburial. This scene would be repeated in Indian country throughout the years as burial land became desirable real estate.

From left to right, John Longfred, Mary Shipman, Ann Hiaton, and Catherine McLeod Mounts chat at the Longfred home at the old Nisqually Agency, located on present-day Fort Lewis. John Longfred was Mary Shipman's second husband. Mary, a basket maker, was allotted land on the Nisqually Reservation through her first husband, James Shipman, who was Nisqually. Ann Hiaton was the wife of John Hiaton, who signed the Medicine Creek Treaty and was also a medicine man. Catherine McLeod was the daughter of a full-blooded Nisqually woman known as Mary. Her uncle Tyee Dick signed the Medicine Creek Treaty. Catherine married Daniel Mounts, an American who worked at the Nisqually Agency as a farmer. Catherine McLeod Mounts collected baskets, many of which are now in museum collections. (Courtesy McBride-Schneider.)

Parson before he was a Parson

Harts Lake Loop Road in Roy, Washington, seen around 1900, was part of the original 2.3 million acres of Nisqually lands between Mount Rainier and Puget Sound. Nisqually went to war because the Medicine Creek Treaty (1854) left the Nisqually only 160 acres of poor land away from their river.

Chief John Steilacoom was Annie Steilacoom's husband. The couple lived at the mouth of Chambers Creek in a houseboat. Most South Sound Indians are related and some Steilacoom, Cowlitz, Puyallup, and Squaxin people are now enrolled Nisquallies, having met the requirement for enrollment set by the Nisqually tribe.

Treaty-era pioneer Ezra Meeker first saw the treaty tree in 1894 guided by Chief Steilacoom. Meeker described the visit in a letter to historian Clarence Bagley (left) in 1919. Specific trees, rivers, and land formations served as physical reminders of important events in Indian history. The destruction of land formations meant a loss of devices used to pass down Indian history. (Courtesy University of Washington Libraries.)

This image, like most early photographs, was initially a stereo view, commercially sold as a set for education and entertainment in the United States. Some Indian people were paid a fee for their photographs; others, perhaps like Annie Steilacoom, were not asked permission. The old Russian blue bead strands around her neck may have been added by the photographer for a more "Indian" look. (Courtesy McBride-Schneider.)

Romantic images of cedar bark–clad natives and Mount Rainier were popular parlor room decorations at the dawn of the 20th century. This 1911 oil painting by Tacoma artist and photographer Albert Henry Barnes depicts Mount Rainier as seen from Vashon Island. (Courtesy Washington State Historical Society.)

Henry Sicade (born 1866), a Puyallup/Nisqually, was a graduate of Forest Grove Indian and Industrial Training School and returned to Tacoma to become a successful and influential businessman. His father was Charlie Sicade, a Nisqually, and his mother was Susan Stann, a Puyallup/Nisqually. Throughout his life, Sicade expressed a strong interest in Indian culture, and he wrote short articles about Indian life. Sicade was an active member of the Republican party, helped assess condemned reservation lands on present-day Fort Lewis, and advocated education as a way for Indians to better themselves.

This sketch depicts Fort Nisqually as it may have looked in 1843. The original fort was set on a bank overlooking the Nisqually River and was later rebuilt on the more desirable Nisqually Prairie. The fort stood on prime Indian land. Hudson's Bay Company squatted on vast areas of traditional gathering grounds for cattle and sheep farms. Later the Americans would pay the British compensation for improvements on Indian land. (Courtesy Archives of British Columbia, Victoria, British Columbia.)

Photographs like these of Nelson and his wife, both Puyallup, were sold as souvenirs to tourists. The couple stands in front of a lean-to structure on their land around 1890. Nelson fought in the Treaty Wars when South Sound tribes all looked to Leschi for leadership. Nelson was accused of killing settlers in the White River Valley.

44

Some Hudson's Bay Company employees became American citizens after the United States gained permanent control of the South Sound in 1843. Edward Huggins's home was the last structure left on the old Fort Nisqually site. Huggins became an American citizen and filed preemption papers on the fort property. Edward Huggins lived out his life in Tacoma, investing in real estate and working at a bank. Huggins left journals, letters, and newspaper articles that describe early interactions with Indian people. He knew Chief Leschi and his wives.

Washington's first territorial governor, Gen. Isaac Ingalls Stevens, was at heart a soldier. He graduated with honors from West Point Military Academy, spent many years in the military, and died on the battlefield during the Civil War. Stevens is remembered as the first territorial governor of Washington, as well as the man who negotiated the treaties that transferred Indian land in present-day Washington to the United States. Stevens was also responsible for the hanging of Chief Leschi. In this portrait, done prior to 1853, Stevens wears a buckskin jacket (perhaps a gift) crisscrossed with Métis beaded embroidery, probably the straps to bandoliers or shoulder bags. Stevens also holds a pipe, a symbol of negotiation in Indian country. (Courtesy Washington State Historical Society.)

Simon Plomondon, a French Canadian Hudson's Bay Company employee, settled in the Cowlitz area and married Thas-o-muth, a daughter of headman Schanawah and sister of Leschi's fellow soldier, Tyee Dick. Plomondon counts descendants in many tribes, including the Cowlitz, Nisqually, and Quinault.

Daniel Mounts was the agency farmer on the Nisqually Reservation. He married Catherine ("Kitty") McLeod, the daughter of Hudson's Bay Company employee John McLeod and Mary. Historian Edward Huggins in 1901 wrote that Daniel Mounts said that his wife's mother, Mary—a full-blooded Nisqually—had been stolen by Vancouver Island Indians as a girl. Mary was rescued by an English family in Victoria and met her future husband, John McLeod, on her return trip home on board the *Beaver*. Del McBride, Mary's descendant, became an artist and a museum curator in Spokane and Olympia. (Courtesy McBride-Schneider.)

Nancy Jim Parsons (born 1871) was of Cowlitz/Nisqually ancestry. At the age of 21, she married John Parsons, who was the son of a Nisqually mother and a white father, William F. Parsons. Nancy Jim Parsons made coiled and imbricated baskets, and as she had no children, many were given to her close friend Catherine Mounts.

Basket maker Nancy Parsons died of cancer in 1918. Here she wears a headband and an abalone button at the neck of her stylish dress. Note she is in the same dress as on the previous page. (Courtesy McBride-Schneider.)

Mary Longfred, widow of Nisqually James Shipman and wife of Johnny Longfred, wears the brightly colored striped skirt and straw hat that were favored by Indian women and were often criticized by "proper" white ladies as being too loud. (Courtesy McBride-Schneider.)

Catherine McLeod Mounts (seated), Christina Mounts (left), and John Mounts (right) are pictured here around 1870. Catherine and Christina wear dentalia or shell money necklaces in this portrait. The shell necklaces indicated high status in Indian society while the stylish western clothes and hairstyles were markers of high status in American society. (Courtesy McBride-Schneider.)

Mary Longfred, with a white apron at left, stands with Catherine Mounts (to her right), and Johnny Longfred (in front) on the Quinault Reservation. Two young family members or friends pose with them. Many Nisqually and Cowlitz received allotments of land on the Quinault Reservation. (Courtesy McBride-Schneider.)

Aunt Jane, a Nisqually basket maker (seated), poses with her daughter Martha. Jane was married to a Hawaiian Hudson's Bay Company employee around 1860. The hair of the Indian dog seated at Jane's feet was worked into the wool during Salish blanket weaving. (Courtesy McBride-Schneider.)

Old Steilacoom, who worked for Daniel Mounts, is pictured near a shack on the Mounts property at the mouth of the Nisqually River. The shack was a temporary structure Steilacoom used while fishing. (Courtesy McBride-Schneider.)

"Ol Steilacoom"

Sam Mounts, grandson of Catherine Mounts, poses in what may be one of Nancy Parson's baskets around 1905. Catherine Mounts is one of the few Indian women who was able to collect and preserve the basketry traditions of the first people of Washington. German anthropologist Hermann Haeberlin interviewed her in 1916–1917 about Nisqually traditions. (Courtesy McBride-Schneider.)

Pioneers consulted John Hiaton (right) on many matters. A controversy among the non-Indian citizenry in Tacoma regarding the true name of Tacobet (Mount Rainier) meant Hiaton was asked for his recall on the subject. Hiaton's wife sits below him wearing a scarf smartly tied around her neck. Olympia Jim, wearing a hat, is on Hiaton's left. Jim's wife sits below him.

John Hiaton, Nisqually treaty signer, poses in his medicine man robe around 1900. Among the Nisqually, both men and women could be healers. Some sought these powers and others inherited them. Hiaton lived on the Puyallup Reservation.

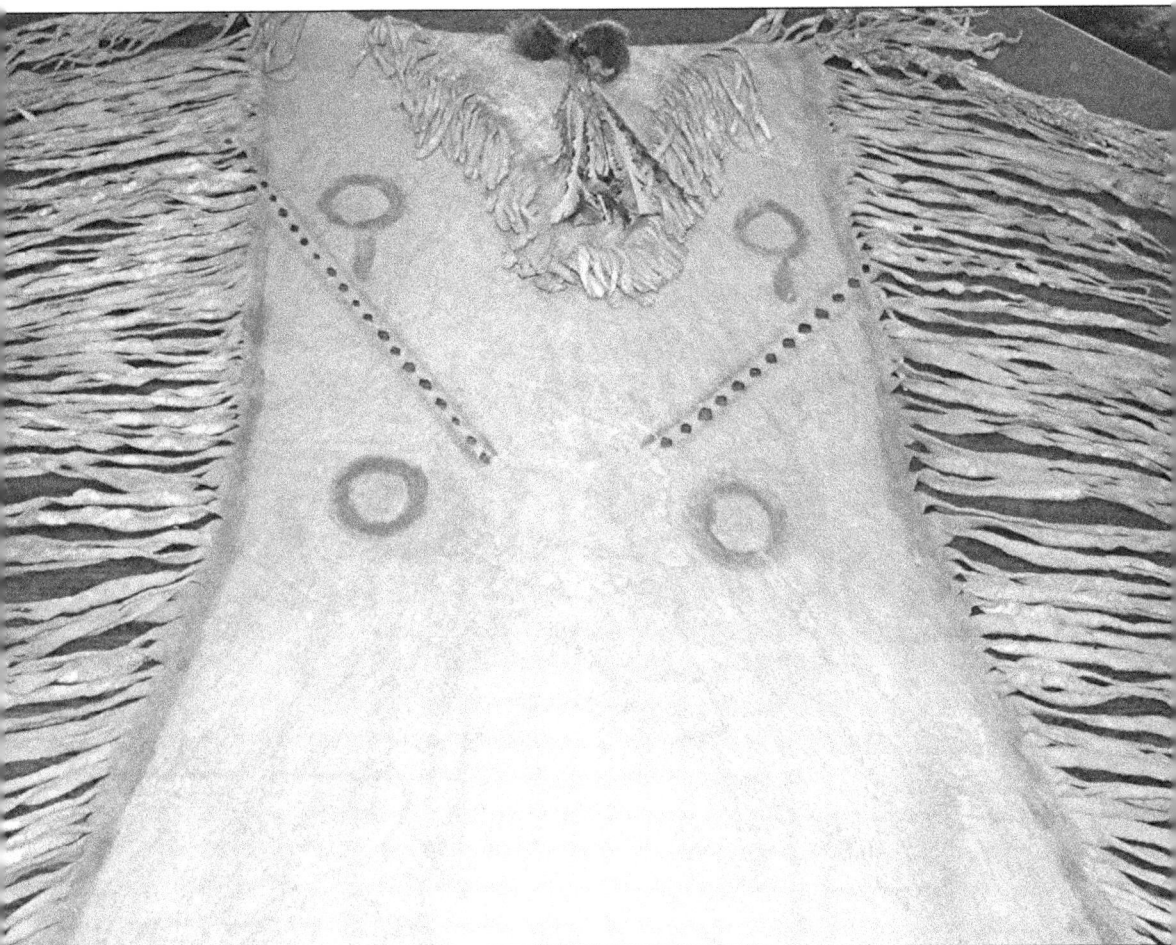

John Hiaton's medicine man robe was located in New York in 2005 and is now back in the Northwest. Loose abstract imagery, like that on the robe, is often associated with the spirit world. (Courtesy Curtright and Son Tribal Art.)

Mapmaking for the Americans was a prelude to possession of the land. William H. Carlton drew this map of Indian country under the direction of Isaac Stevens, who was territorial governor, head of the railroad survey, and superintendent of Indian affairs. It details the location of the different tribes.

Two

LESCHI'S PEOPLE

This 1935 photograph taken at the Peter Kalama family home shows anthropologist Marian Smith, kneeling in a suit at right. On either side of her stand the Kalama twins—Zelma and Zelda. The twins, like their father, grew up to take leadership positions in the Nisqually community. The elderly gentleman with a white moustache (back row, center) is Henry Martin, the Nisqually leader who often acted as interpreter for the tribe. Marian Smith wrote *The Puyallup-Nisqually*, the essential early history of the Nisqually.

The most extensive paper archive on the Nisqually is located in the basement at the home of Nisqually historian Cecelia Carpenter in Parkland, Washington. Carpenter began gathering the written history of the tribe in 1960 by visiting local historical societies and archives across the nation.

Historian Cecelia Carpenter married at age 17, raised a family, and then returned to school. Her master's thesis was on the treaty and fishing rights of her Nisqually people.

Rev. H. N. Svinth poses on a thickly wooded road headed to Mount Rainier, or Tacobet. With his wife, Mary Edna, a Nisqually woman, he farmed near Harts Lake Loop Road in Roy, which was originally Nisqually land. Nisqually lived on the reservation as well as in the surrounding towns and cities.

George Brown and his wife, Annie, are described as Puyallup because they resided on the Puyallup Reservation. But most reservations were home to differing tribes. Indian-ness became a rigid legal category when the federal government requested that tribes prepare lists of enrolled members in the 1930s.

George Leschi, nephew of Chief Leschi, poses in pseudo-Indian garb for the Mitchell Portrait Studio in Puyallup, Washington, around 1890. Photographers often had costumes that could be used to give local Indians the authentic feel desired by tourists who collected photographs and stereo views. Some Indian people considered it one more way to make extra money.

TREATY COMES HOME

In Washington for the first time since 1854: the Medicine Creek treaty that still shapes U.S./Indian relations here.

Portrait of George Leschi, Nisqually, a child when the treaty was signed.

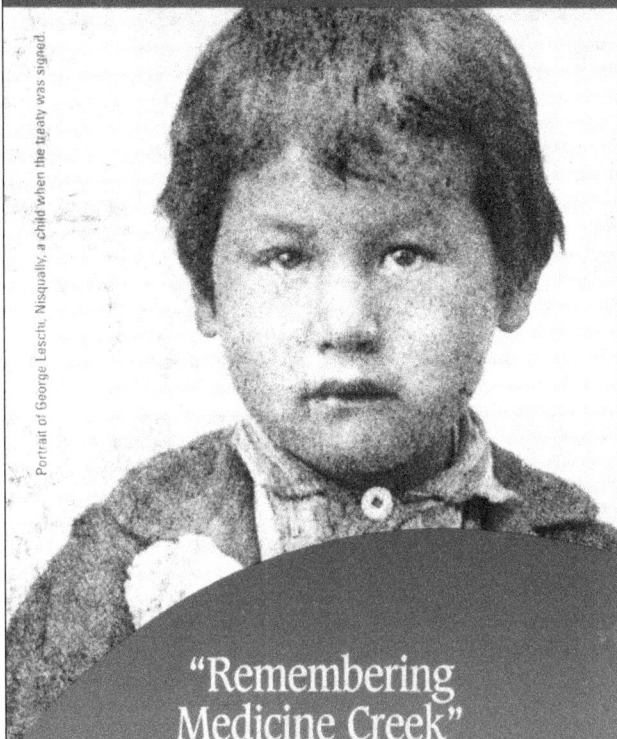

"Remembering Medicine Creek"
at the Washington State History Museum

October 17, 1998 - January 10, 1999

The Washington State History Museum is in downtown Tacoma 2 minutes off Interstate 5 (exit 133) with its own parking lot.

Don't miss the 25,000 square feet of other exciting exhibits. For more information call toll free 1-888-BE-THERE.

WASHINGTON STATE HISTORICAL SOCIETY

1911 Pacific Avenue, Tacoma, WA 98402

George Leschi's portrait as a child advertised Remembering Medicine Creek, a 5,000-square-foot exhibit on the colonization of the South Sound, the Medicine Creek Treaty, the Indian wars, and the revitalization of Indian reserved rights in the state. The heart of the exhibit was the actual treaty, which was lent by the National Archives in Washington, D.C. This was the first time the treaty had returned to Washington State. Cecelia Carpenter and Maria Pascualy were curators of the exhibit, which was held in 1998 at the Washington State History Museum in Tacoma, Washington.

Paul Leschi, a direct descendant of Quaymuth (Leschi's brother), served as chair of the Election Board when the Nisqually Constitution was adopted. Wade Vaughn, who took this photograph, interviewed 87-year-old Leschi in 1976. Leschi provided details of life on the Pierce County side of the reservation. His descendant Cynthia Iyall was elected chair of the Nisqually tribe in 2006.

Frank Iyall, seated at the table, fourth from the left, helped craft the Indian Citizenship Act of 1924 that granted citizenship to all Indians. He is the great-grandfather of Nisqually chair Cynthia Iyall, pictured below. (Courtesy Iyall family.)

Nisqually tribal members met before the exoneration of Chief Leschi in 2004 at the House of Representatives in Olympia. In this photograph are (first row) Nisqually tribal chair Dorian Sanchez (fourth from the right); Cynthia Iyall, present Nisqually chair (second from right); and Albert Iyall (far right); (center background) Jimmy McCloud, wearing a cedar bark headband and holding a picture of Leschi. Tribal members argued that the territorial government judicially murdered Leschi after the Treaty Wars and eventually won his exoneration. Leschi was the first person in Washington to be executed by the government.

Longtime head of the Indian Fisheries Commission, Billy Frank Jr. and his wife, Redwing, a journalist, pose with Cecelia Carpenter (left), historian, and Georgeanna Kautz, fisheries manager, as they celebrate Billy's 75th birthday. Frank was a key player in the fish-ins that led to the Boldt Decision.

Lorna Kalama and Gary Hicks pose with a carving of Chief Leschi made by Danny Murphy in 1991. For years, the tribe kept Chief Leschi's memory alive through stories, ceremonies, exhibits, and talking about him in the community whenever possible. In 2005, years of work by the Nisqually community culminated in his exoneration.

Georgeanna Kautz (left), Nisqually Tribal and Natural Resources manager, tracks the fish runs in the Nisqually River and decides when fishermen can fish. She poses with her sister, Ramona, who holds a contemporary coiled basket. The Washington State Historical Society holds the largest collection of Nisqually material culture.

Ground-breaking for the tribal center built in 1977 meant an end to renting meeting space off reservation. Georgeanna Kautz (left), tribal chair in 1977, poses with past chair Zelma McCloud. From the beginning, Nisqually women did the day-to-day hard work that moved the tribe toward economic independence. Many of their stories are unwritten.

Willie Frank Sr. (center), father of
Nisqually leader Billy Frank, poses with
Indian rights activist Allison Bridges
Gottfriedson (left) and Maureen Yvonne
Frank at the 1977 ground-breaking for
the new tribal center. Allison, as well as
her sisters Suzette and Valerie, put their
lives at risk during the fishing wars of
the 1960s. The architect's drawing for
the tribal center is in the background.

Zelma Kalama McCloud (right) led the
Nisqually tribe during the lean years of
the 1960s and 1970s as chair. She poses
with vice chair Cecelia Carpenter and
U.S. congressman Don Bonkers. McCloud
participated in the ground-breaking of the
long-sought-after tribal center. Prior to this
event, Nisqually tribal headquarters were in
rented buildings in Yelm, Washington. As of
2007, McCloud continues to serve the tribe
in her senior capacity.

Alice Kalama started the Nisqually Indian Church on Kalama Road after the two other churches were destroyed. The church served as the meeting place for the tribal council until the new center was built in 1977.

Zelda Kalama Thompson is the twin sister of Zelma Kalama McCloud. Both sisters grew up to be active tribal members, with Zelma holding the tribal chairmanship several times.

George Kalama, son of Roy Kalama, served in Vietnam and like many Nisqually was a veteran. Indian men served in the military even before recognition as American citizens in 1924. Kalama, who raised the funds for the Nisqually tribal center, sadly drowned while fishing on the Nisqually River.

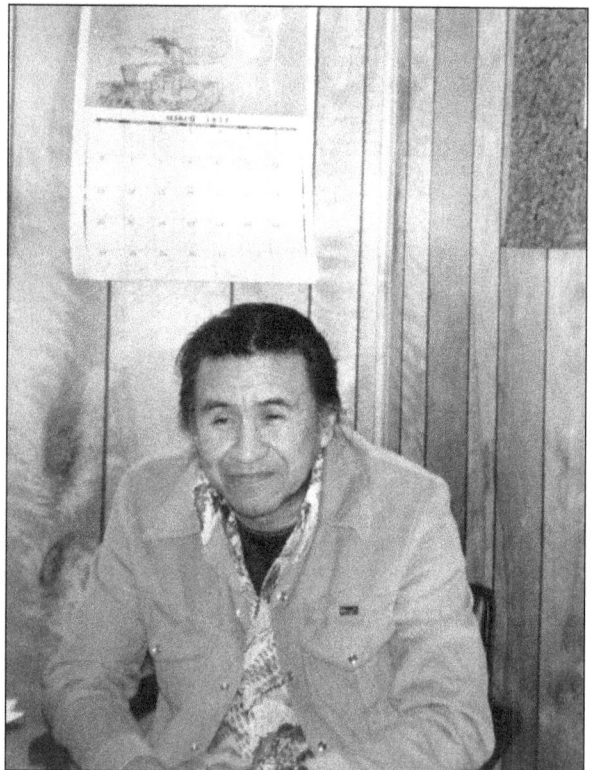

Pictured here in 1977, Billy Frank Jr. (Nisqually) has been director of the Northwest Fisheries Commission for over 30 years. The commission is the steward of salmon for the benefit of all people in Washington.

Lucille Ledoux served as business manager of the Nisqually tribe in the 1970s. She later studied law and served as a tribal judge. Serving in government often inspired Nisqually men and women to pursue higher education so as to better help the tribe.

The Nisqually Indian Tribe
cordially invites you to attend
the Dedication of the
Nisqually Indian Bingo
on the Nisqually Indian Reservation
on Wednesday, August 5, 1992.

The Open House will be from
12:00 - 5:00 p.m.

The Nisqually Tribal Chairman, Dorian Sanchez
will give the Welcome Speech at 12:30
followed by tours and free refreshments.

Grand Opening will be August 7, 1992.

NISQUALLY INDIAN
BINGO

The Nisqually tribe has an economic development arm charged with making the tribe self-sufficient for the good of the people. The bingo hall, which opened in 1992, is the precursor of the highly successful Red Wind Casino. Profits from the casino help fund social services in the community.

The highway sign for the Red Wind Casino is the most prominent marker on the Nisqually Reservation, located 15 miles to the east of Olympia, Washington. The success of the casino means elders receive additional economic assistance from the tribe and that youth can benefit from educational programs and social services.

Gambling has always been part of intertribal gatherings in Indian country, even today. Indian hops pickers in Puyallup in the 1880s shared news and food and competed through gambling. Today Nisqually staff runs a casino used mostly by non-Indians. (Courtesy Washington State Historical Society.)

In 1931, Ruby McAllister's class at the Nisqually School District included the following Nisqually children: Leo Sanchez (No. 11), Wilfred Kover (No. 12), Ted Kover (No. 14), Alice Sanchez (No. 24), Margie Gleason (No. 29), Betty Gleason (No. 31), and Buck Johns (No. 32). Most of these children stayed in the area and have descendants living on reservation lands. Ruby McAllister was of Cowlitz/Quinault ancestry.

Mary (left) and Cecelia Svinth, both Nisqually, inherited the Danish features of their father. The importance of "looking Indian" increased with the Indian pride movement of the 1960s.

Logging was a means of employment for men in the South Sound, both Indian and non-Indian. Great wealth accumulated in the state from the sale and processing of what were once Indian resources. This young man, a Nisqually, takes a break at a mill during the Second World War.

The Indian pride movement that began in the 1960s meant many families now felt safe publicly reclaiming their Indian heritage. Four Nisqually brothers and sisters of the Svinth family pose at their home in Roy, Washington, in 1930. From left to right, Ruth married a Sioux man and moved to Minnesota, Mary became a housewife in Washington State, Cecelia became active in Nisqually tribal politics and then dedicated her life to researching the history of the Nisqually, and Paul attended Chemawa Indian School in Oregon and then joined the military.

Mary Edna Svinth (Nisqually) chats with Bertha Westlin (Quinault). Westlin stood up for Willie Frank (Nisqually) at his wedding. Marriages and births were always intertribal celebrations because the community was and is small (enrolled Nisqually only number about 500), and everyone was a friend or a relative.

This postcard was sold in the gift shop of the Cushman Indian Hospital in 1950, which served Indians from Alaska, Oregon, Washington, and Montana with tuberculosis or other diseases. (Courtesy Washington State Historical Society.)

Baseball in the 1920s was played in the field across from Frank's Landing in Nisqually. Later intertribal games were also played on the present site of the Fort Lewis Golf Club off Mounts Road in Nisqually. The Nisqually Archives staff is in the process of identifying the team members in this 1929 photograph. (Courtesy Nisqually Indian Tribe Archive.)

Frank Iyall, born in 1876, lobbied for the rights of the Nisqually, Yakama, and Cowlitz tribes in Washington, D.C. His mother was Margaret O'Powety, daughter of Nisqually headman and hunter O'Powety who was born in 1800. (Courtesy Nisqually Indian Tribe Archive.)

Nisqually children formed a large part of the McAllister School in the Nisqually Valley around 1900. Approximately 12,000 Indian men, including some of these boys, served during World War I. (Courtesy Nisqually Indian Tribe Archive.)

The News ⛬ Tribune

9₁ST YEAR, NO. 232　　　　TACOMA, WASH.　　Final　　TUESDAY, FEBRUARY 12, 1974　　TEN CENTS

Court gives Indians priority fishing rights

By JACK WILKINS
News Tribune Staff Writer

Federal Judge George H. Boldt ruled here Tuesday in an historically important and long-awaited decision that current Washington State fishing regulations are unlawful when applied to 14 "treaty" Indian tribes.

He ruled, in effect, that after preservation of fish runs to ensure survival, the treaty Indians come first in fishing rights.

And Boldt put his court into a watchdog role in regard to disputes over those rights, saying the court will retain jurisdiction of the case.

Soon, the judge said, he will schedule a hearing to determine whether he should "appoint a master with technical fisheries expertise to assist the court in helping the parties to reach agreed solutions of problems." The hearing also will consider whether the court should appoint an advisory committee on the subject.

THE CASE WAS brought in 1970 by the federal government, on behalf of itself and the tribes including the Puyallup and the Nisqually. The government sought to have the court force the state fisheries and game departments set regulations recognizing treaty-guaranteed special fishing rights.

The judge did so Tuesday, after a month of concentrated work on the anthropological, historical, biological and legal evidence and arguments presented in court last fall.

Boldt carried forward — and but sharpened — a 1968 U.S. Supreme Court decision that declared certain Indians to have special fishing rights. But he also stated that the state has the right to regulate those rights in the interests of conservation.

Boldt's decision reverberated with language of the Isaac I. Stevens treaties of the 1850s with various of the tribes. Those are treaties whose subsequent interpretations by local, state and federal courts have muddied the fishing-rights picture for 50 years.

THE JUDGE NOTED that the treaties gave fishing rights to Indians in their usual and accustomed places "in common with" other citizens of the territory. And he ruled that the phrase "does not secure any treaty right or privilege to anyone other than the treaty tribes. . . ."

He declared that the phrase operates "only to limit the exercise of the tribes'

Staff photo by Jerry Buck

Judge Boldt based decision on voluminous study

The 1974 Boldt Decision, which upheld Nisqually reserved rights to fish off reservation in their usual and accustomed places, is still not well understood by outsiders. Indians were not given priority rights by the U.S. government; rather they signed a contract, a treaty that is legally binding, in which they reserved certain lands and rights in perpetuity. (Courtesy *Tacoma News Tribune*.)

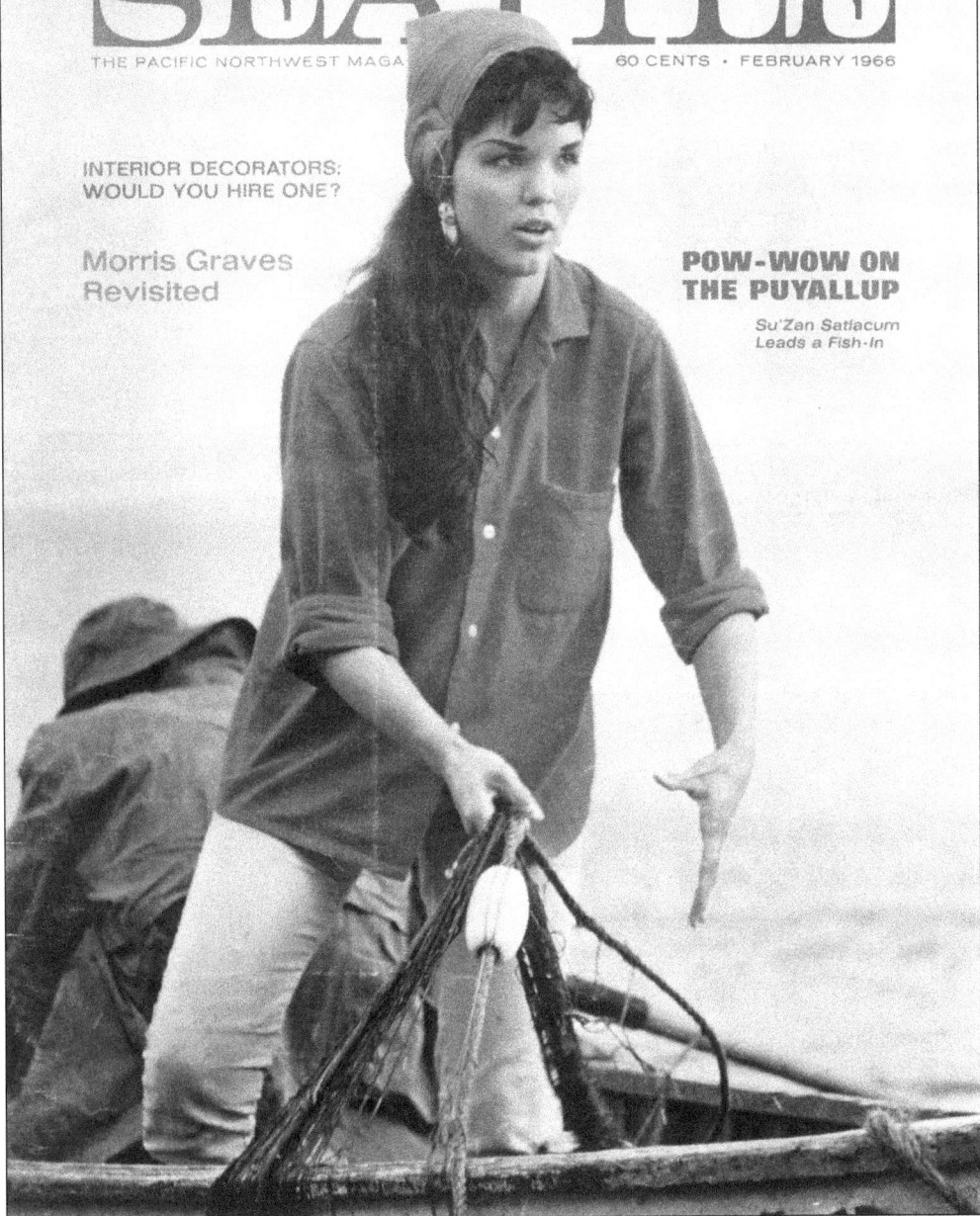

SuZan Satiacum, second wife of Indian rights activist Robert Satiacum, is the cover girl for fishing rights on the February 1966 issue of the fashionable *Seattle* magazine. Her interview includes descriptions of violence on the Nisqually River, divisions among tribal members regarding strategy, and a strong passion for justice regarding fishing rights. The story of Indian women in the fish wars has yet to be told. (Courtesy *Seattle* magazine.)

The construction of Fort Lewis destroyed Indian homes as well as the homes of whites. Greendale was a white town that disappeared with the establishment of Fort Lewis.

Historian Arthur Ballard photographed storyteller and Treaty Wars soldier Nisqually Charlie and his wife in 1917 after the condemnation of the Nisqually land on the Pierce County side. The photograph was archived at the Smithsonian with a letter from Ballard describing their perilous living situation. (Courtesy National Anthropological Archives, neg. INV00022200.)

The 115th Cavalry parades where Leschi once trained his troops during the Treaty Wars. From 1917 to 1918, Fort Lewis was established by absorbing two-thirds of Nisqually reserved lands. Today an Iraqi village called Leschi-town covers the area and is used for combat practice by the army.

Nisqually Mary Edna Svinth, 17 and married, poses with a book at her family home. She was the granddaughter of Catherine Ross, wife of Charley Ross, who was allotted land on the Nisqually Indian Reservation.

Sam P'yelo poses in the snub-nose dugout canoe preferred by Indians when traveling on inland waters. The middle section of the Nisqually homelands was too thickly forested for easy travel by foot. P'yelo, who knew the waters well, was paid to ferry outsiders from place to place as well as to transport goods. (Courtesy University of Washington Libraries.)

Sam P'yelo was part Hawaiian, as were many other Nisqually who were children of Hawaiian fathers in the employ of the Hudson's Bay Company. P'yelo fought in the Treaty Wars with Leschi, and in later years, he had a canoe ferry at the mouth of Muck Creek. (Courtesy University of Washington Libraries.)

The McLeod-Mounts clan, an international pioneer family, poses in front of the Mounts home in Nisqually, Washington, around 1894. Daniel Mounts, the American-born Nisqually Agency farmer, holds his daughter in his lap and sits next to his father-in-law, Scotsman John McLeod. McLeod was one of the Hudson's Bay Company men who lived on Muck Creek and defied territorial governor Isaac Stevens during the treaty wars. His oldest daughter, Catherine Mounts, sits at far left. Catherine McLeod was the daughter of a Cowlitz/Nisqually woman known as Mary. Catherine's daughter Christina, who suffered from cataracts, sits at far right with daughter Pauline in her lap. Children and grandchildren surround the family patriarch. John McLeod still has descendants on the Nisqually Reservation who spell their name McCloud, and among them is Georgeanna Kautz, who is fisheries manager for the Nisqually Indian Tribe. (Courtesy McBride-Schneider.)

Gift giving and the sharing of food is commonplace across Indian country, even today. This photograph documents what was described as the last big giveaway held at a ranch near Alderton, Washington, around 1907. Traditional foods were served with more modern foods. Dried salmon hangs above the woman on the left.

Youngsters were posed for this promotional picture of the Chemawa Indian School in Salem, Oregon. Students from Nisqually attended the school that today still runs at full capacity. (Courtesy Oregon Historical Society.)

Forest Grove Indian Training School opened with an entire class from the Puyallup Reservation School. Some Chemawa graduates, like Puyallup Peter Stanup (seated, second from right) and Nisqually Henry Sicade (second row, left), became successful businessmen and agreed with the sale of allotted lands. Nisqually Peter Kalama (first row, center) came home and worked to represent the claims and rights of his people in court. (Courtesy Oregon Historical Society.)

Francis W. Cushman, a congressman from Tacoma, championed the Puyallup Indian School, which he used to show outsiders the progress of Indians in his state. The school was later renamed after him. Nisqually children attended the Puyallup Indian School. Henry Sicade, who supported the work of his alma mater Chemawa (originally Forest Grove Indian School), criticized the teachers and training at Puyallup.

Paul Svinth (Nisqually) attended Chemawa Indian School and served as student body president in 1943. He also served in the U.S. Army until his death. The warrior tradition continued in Indian country as students from Cushman Indian School enlisted during World War II and continued the tradition throughout all subsequent wars.

In 1889, St. George's Industrial School was one year old. It was a Catholic school for Indians founded by a Belgian priest, Father Hylebos (the priest on the far right wearing a hat), and was run by sisters from the order of St. Francis. St. George's competed with the Indian school on the Puyallup Reservation for students. The school was located between Tacoma and Seattle in the south end of Federal Way. Gethsemane Cemetery encompasses the school grounds today.

Youngsters from the Spokane tribe pose for their picture at Forest Grove Industrial School in Salem, Oregon, in 1882. Girls were trained for domestic service, which was considered a marketable skill, and did the wash and mending for all the students as practice. Despite the hardship of leaving home, some graduates felt the school helped them speak for their tribe and others appreciated the chance to fit more easily into the new society. The school, which was coeducational, was run in a military fashion, and pictures like this were used as promotional material to raise money and show the advancement of the tribes. (Courtesy Curtright and Son Tribal Arts.)

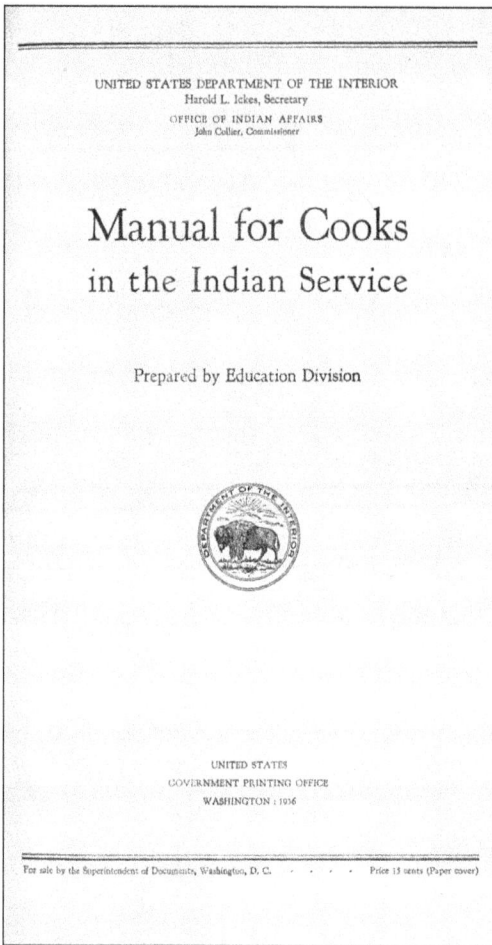

The Bureau of Indian Affairs under John Collier (1933) published special pamphlets dealing with the Indian diet in boarding schools with suggestions on how to introduce less familiar foods to the students. Changes in the traditional diet have led to high levels of diabetes, cancer, and heart disease in Indian country.

UNITED STATES DEPARTMENT OF THE INTERIOR
Harold L. Ickes, Secretary

OFFICE OF INDIAN AFFAIRS
John Collier, Commissioner

Manual for Cooks
in the Indian Service

Prepared by Education Division

UNITED STATES
GOVERNMENT PRINTING OFFICE
WASHINGTON : 1936

For sale by the Superintendent of Documents, Washington, D. C. - - - - Price 15 cents (Paper cover)

Established in 1915, Lacamas Grade School was located on Lacamas Creek, seven miles east of Roy, and served Nisqually Reservation children as well as other students.

Edna Binder (foreground left) married Hans Svinth in a traditional service in 1903. Nisqually leader Henry Martin (third from right), with a white handlebar moustache, was an honored guest at the event.

Henry Martin (Nisqually) served as interpreter in several important court cases. It was a great blow to the tribe when Martin died during the condemnation of the Pierce County side of the reservation. Martin ran a canoe ferry service on the lower Nisqually River as a young man. (Courtesy University of Washington Libraries.)

Henry Martin (second from left) represented Nisqually at intertribal events. Here he is a witness at the marriage of Ed Smith (Chehalis) at Mud Bay, Olympia. Olympia Jim (far left) and Mary Jackson Jim (far right in the broad hat) are also in attendance.

Father Blanchet, a French Canadian missionary, brought the Catholic religion to Nisqually country in 1839. Indian people were tolerant of all religions and tended to layer the new teachings onto their old spiritual beliefs. Many years later, a Catholic church, St. Anthony's, was established on the reservation and served about 30 Catholic parishioners. St. Anthony's was demolished when two-thirds of Nisqually land was condemned to build Fort Lewis.

John Hote (or Xot), now blind, sits at home with his wife, Mary, a niece of Chief Seattle. Hote's father, Chief Chee-Chap-Witch, signed the Medicine Creek Treaty. Historian Arthur Ballard collected Hote's stories, including one about Fox Island where the Nisqually were interned at the end of the Treaty Wars. (Courtesy University of Washington Libraries.)

A group of Tacoma businessmen and historians mark the spot where Chief Leschi was hung outside the gates of Fort Steilacoom. Frank Stone (in the car) and W. P. Bonney (third from left) were both representatives of the Washington State Historical Society. Bonney, who was born at Steilacoom, later wrote a three-volume history of Pierce County.

NISQUALLY

HERE, IN THE NISQUALLY VALLEY, ON THE BANK OF MᶜALLISTER CREEK, ALSO KNOWN AS MEDICINE CREEK AND BY THE INDIANS CALLED SHE-NAH-NAM, IS THE MEMORABLE SPOT WHERE ISAAC I. STEVENS, FIRST TERRITORIAL GOVERNOR OF WASHINGTON, SAT IN COUNSEL WITH THE CHIEFTAINS OF THE LOWER PUGET SOUND INDIAN TRIBES, PRINCIPALLY THE NISQUALLYS, PUYALLUPS AND SQUAXONS, DECEMBER 24 TO 26, 1854. THE RESULTING MEDICINE CREEK TREATY PURCHASED LAND FOR WHITE SETTLERS, AWARDED RESERVATIONS TO THE INDIANS, AND CONCLUDED THE FIRST IN A SERIES OF IMPORTANT NORTHWEST INDIAN TREATIES.

This highway marker, now removed, marked the spot where the Medicine Creek Treaty was signed in 1854. Note the Plains Indian headdress on what is purported to be a South Sound Indian negotiating the treaty.

Three

PEOPLE OF THE TREATY

Frank Iyall, third from the right, poses for a formal portrait with other tribal leaders at the signing of the 1924 Indian Citizenship Act in Washington, D.C. Although still not considered citizens at birth, most Indians by this time had already attained citizenship through allotment, marriage to citizens, or military service. (Courtesy Iyall family.)

Hops rest on the umbrella used to keep the sun off this Nisqually baby on the Pincus farm around 1900. Nisqually families picked hops into the early 1960s. Joe Kalama, Nisqually archives manager, is leading a project to identify people in Nisqually photographs like this one. (Courtesy Nisqually Indian Tribe Archive.)

Lizzie Frank John, right, stands in a hop field and holds Margaret John in her arms. Willie Frank, father of Nisqually leader and visionary Billy Frank, stands behind her in a striped sweater and hat. Sally Jackson, a healer, wears a large headscarf and stands directly next to them, holding a hop vine. The others are probably members of the Kalama family, pictured in 1900. (Courtesy Nisqually Indian Tribe Archive.)

Rose McCloud, far right, stands on the back porch with her daughters. Her descendants hold positions of authority on the Nisqually and Puyallup Reservations. (Courtesy Nisqually Indian Tribe Archive.)

Alma Gleason, fourth from left, poses with friends in this *c.* 1925 Nisqually Dance Troupe portrait. The Gleason family has long been active in tribal politics. (Courtesy Nisqually Indian Tribe Archive.)

George McCloud Sr. served in the U.S. Army during World War I. He came back to Nisqually and raised a family of 13 children. He was born on the condemned Pierce County side of the Nisqually Reservation. (Courtesy Nisqually Indian Tribe Archive.)

George McCloud Jr., son of George McCloud, followed in his father's footsteps and served in the military during World War II along with 40,000 other Indian servicemen. (Courtesy Nisqually Indian Tribe Archive.)

Ernest Gleason poses in his US. Army uniform during World War II. He played on the Nisqually intertribal baseball team in the 1930s. (Courtesy Nisqually Indian Tribe Archive.)

Robert Sison is a Nisqually elder and U.S. Navy veteran of the Korean War. Chief Leschi and his soldiers are considered the first Nisqually veterans. The Nisqually tribe estimates that more than 100 men have died defending the United States during wartime. (Courtesy Nisqually Indian Tribe Archive.)

Margaret Davis Weeskas (left), Gladys Davis, and Elsie Squally Thomas pose in their hop-picking clothes, probably on the Pincus farm, around 1920. An unidentified man stands behind the girls. (Courtesy Nisqually Indian Tribe Archive.)

Alice Kalama, wife of Peter Kalama, stands inside her home at Christmas. She worked shoulder to shoulder with her husband, Nisqually leader Peter Kalama. Although most heads of villages were men, there were one or two accounts of women chiefs among the Nisqually in the early days.

Nisqually leader Peter Kalama (born 1860), husband of Alice Kalama, led the tribe during the loss of two-thirds of tribal lands with the establishment of Fort Lewis. For many years, natural leaders, many educated at Chemawa in white ways, represented the tribe. Later, with the development of a formal constitution, elected officers were appointed to fulfill specific duties within the tribe. Kalama was a descendant of a Hawaiian employee of the Hudson's Bay Company, John Kalama (born 1814), who married an Indian woman, Mary Martin. His daughter Zelma Kalama said her father used his expertise to help other tribes receive justice in courts. Their home was a stopping ground for political discussion.

97

Antoine Jackson was a Nisqually leader of Hawaiian ancestry. Hawaii was a wintering over place for the Hudson's Bay Company ships and crews, and starting in 1811, Hawaiians were recruited to work for the company. Due to disease and economic hardship at home, over 500 Hawaiian men eventually migrated to the Northwest coast, most marrying into indigenous communities.

Sally Jackson, wife of Antoine Jackson, was a medicine woman, or shaman. She was said to cure by rubbing her hands over the wounded or painful area. Jackson lost her land after the Nisqually land condemnation in 1917.

Mary Kiona (born 1868), a Cowlitz, was a famed basket maker. Cowlitz people would not sign a treaty with the U.S. government and give up their land, so they were not recognized until 2002. Through the years, some Cowlitz who were close to the Nisqually through marriage or resided on the reservation joined the Nisqually tribe.

Indians and non-Indians gather on the Tacoma waterfront around 1890 to talk and trade. Indians might purchase pans, stoves, or cloth, while outsiders might buy baskets or fresh-caught salmon. In western Washington, Indian people had reservation lands but were not confined to them. Moreover, during boom times, Indian wageworkers were as necessary as any other.

Jimmy Dillon stands on a wooden footbridge around 1950 and takes a snapshot. Dillon played baseball on the Nisqually baseball team in the late 1920s. The Dillon family has relatives on the Nisqually and the Puyallup Reservations. (Courtesy Nisqually Indian Tribe Archive.)

Joe Kalama, Nisqually archives manager, is heading a project to print and identify the tribe's image collection. These two young Nisqually girls, photographed around 1900, wait to be identified. (Courtesy Nisqually Indian Tribe Archive.)

Salmon and salmon roe were traditionally gathered in the winter, smoked on the beach, and then packed home in baskets according to the old ways. This unidentified elder in western Washington smokes his catch Indian style but takes advantage of metal pans and Western fashion. South Sound elders told anthropologist Hermann Haeberlin in 1917 that traditional dress had not been in use for at least 50 years.

The founding of the Ferry Museum in Tacoma, Washington, in 1891 meant the town had achieved a certain level of sophistication and refinement. Museum curators of the day prized large carved works, and this curator craze for totem poles and massive decorated carvings, in Washington, translated into the mistaken belief that South Sound people made totem poles and elaborate regalia. (Courtesy Washington State Historical Society.)

Si-A-Gut was a well-known Nisqually basket maker whose family originally came from the Cowlitz area. She made coiled and imbricated baskets. Si-A-Gut lived and died on the upper Nisqually, and her work is on display at the Washington State History Museum in Tacoma, Washington.

Tacoma's Ferry Museum, founded in 1891, contained many baskets made by Nisqually women—its collections form part of the Washington State Historical Society. In the early days, Nisqually said that they taught the Klickitat to make their famed coiled baskets. Nisqually also made loosely twined soft baskets. (Courtesy Washington State Historical Society.)

Tyee Mary Leschi's remains were moved in 1924 to the cemetery named after her husband, Chief Leschi, on the Puyallup Reservation. Graves had to be moved when Nisqually land was condemned in Pierce County. Her body rests near that of Joseph Leschi, a two-year-old boy. (Courtesy Washington State Historical Society.)

Reburial for Mary Leschi was on May 23, 1924, at the Puyallup Indian Cemetery. Mary was 85 years of age at her death, having been born in Tenino in Nisqually country. Leschi had three

wives—Sarah, Annie, and Mary. (Courtesy Washington State Historical Society.)

Leschi's sister, also named Tyee Mary, is buried at the Nisqually Indian Cemetery located off Reservation Road. This cemetery holds the remains of most of the Nisqually who originally lived on the Pierce County side of the Nisqually Reservation.

Ella Steve was the daughter of Chief Tommy Lane, who was often described as the last hereditary chief of the Puyallup tribe. She was also sister-in-law to Henry Sicade (Nisqually), who married her sister Alice. Puyallup and Nisqually people are closely tied through blood and friendship.

Del McBride (Cowlitz/Quinault), longtime curator at the State Capital Museum in Olympia, poses in ceremonial garb at an exhibit opening in 1965. McBride was also a descendant of Mary, a Nisqually woman, and Hudson's Bay Company employee John McLeod. An artist and historian, McBride was a great resource for early scholarship on the South Sound. (Courtesy McBride-Schneider.)

Christina Mounts (left) was the daughter of Catherine Mounts and grandmother of museum curator, Del McBride. Christina's recollections of Indian life were used in Archie Binns's novel about the South Sound, *Mighty Mountain* (1940) and in Della Gould Emmons's historical novel *Leschi of the Nisquallies* (1965). Christina weaves a coiled basket decorated with raffia at Ella Steve's home in Marysville around 1935. Ella Steve (right), Puyallup, was a basket maker. (Courtesy McBride-Schneider.)

Cecelia Ross (Nisqually) farmed in Roy with her German husband. The town of Roy, which sits on Nisqually land, was the closest town to the Nisqually Reservation on the Pierce County side. Nisqually lands in Pierce County were condemned by the government and turned into Camp Lewis (present-day Fort Lewis Military Base). Cecelia wears a family necklace she inherited from her great-grandmother Quaton, pictured on page 109.

Indian women married British men as well as other foreigners. Quaton, great-great-grandmother of Nisqually historian Cecelia Carpenter, married Sagohanenchta, or Louis the Iroquois, in 1833. Iroquois men from eastern Canada were highly skilled boatmen employed by Hudson's Bay Company.

Evelyn Iyall, age 12, poses for a formal portrait. Her family lived on the condemned Pierce County side of the Nisqually Reservation. (Courtesy Nisqually Indian Tribe Archive.)

The Nisqually tribe has its own government and police force. They ensure that local laws are obeyed on reservation land. Ben Wright (Puyallup) poses with his policeman's badge in 1919. (Courtesy Curtright and Son Tribal Art.)

In 1916, Henry Sicade (Nisqually) told anthropologist Hermann Haeberlin that 100 years before, many Nisqually had migrated to Quinault. Traditions lasted longer the farther Indian people were from non-Indian communities. Here a Quinault carver poses with an unfinished canoe in his backyard in the 1930s. Access to old growth is necessary in order to have the right dimension wood to make old-style seagoing canoes and plank houses. (Courtesy Curtright and Son Tribal Art.)

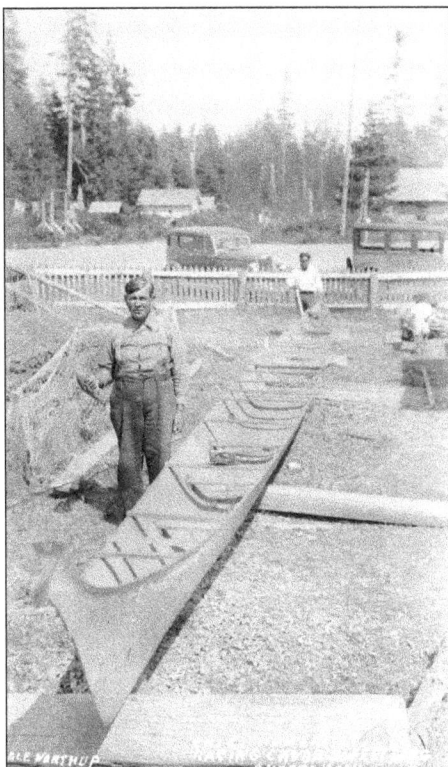

Northwest Indian Fisheries Commission

NEWS

Vol. XV Number 4
Fall 1995

Inside:

- Studying The Marbled Murrelet
- Cooperation Builds Habitat
- Injection Program Protects Fish
- Ancient Tribal Site Revealed
- Shellfish Hatchery Expansion
- New Field Station Opened

The Northwest Indian Fisheries Commission (NWIFC), headed by Billy Frank for the past 30 years, works intertribally for the benefit of the state of Washington and the tribes in a government-to-government relationship. The cover of the 1995 NWIFC newsletter highlights a Skokomish tribal fisherman but also includes scientific reports on the health of chum salmon as well as an update on the Quinault's new field station. Today the newsletter is available on online. (Courtesy Northwest Indian Fisheries Commission.)

111

Intertribal canoe races were held during August in the 1900s on Whidbey Island. Thousands attended the races. (Courtesy Curtright and Son Tribal Art.)

Today Nisqually youth revitalize their culture through the annual intertribal canoe journey. Paddlers travel for two to four weeks, follow a strict no-substance-abuse regime, and work to renew intertribal ties and family friendships. (Courtesy Lou Ann Squally.)

Sturgeon was one of many traditional foods traded into Nisqually country. Although white sturgeon could be found in the estuaries of large rivers like the Nisqually, it was more plentiful on the Columbia River and other places. Sturgeon was harvested in the spring and fall. Isinglass, made from the bladder of the sturgeon, was exported abroad by the Hudson's Bay Company for use in the processing of beer and other foodstuff. This fisherman in Grays Harbor around 1910 prepares to clean his catch. (Courtesy Curtright and Son Tribal Art.)

Hearth stones indicate that a plank house may have existed in this area. Research on the old reservation located at Fort Lewis is unearthing much important history about the Nisqually.

Lillian Iyall Chapell (left), her mother Ida, and sister Mary chat on the family homestead that is located on Reservation Road around 1940. Lillian worked for years at the University of Washington helping students in the American Indian Studies program. (Courtesy Nisqually Indian Tribe Archive.)

Jack Iyall and his wife, Selena Garry Iyall, pictured around 1950, pose on their land. Jack served in the U.S. Navy during World War II. (Courtesy Nisqually Indian Tribe Archive.)

Sara Stomish (left) sits with other traditional women basket makers in front of the Queets Trade Store around 1940. According to Zelma McCloud, a Nisqually elder, traditional women in the 1940s always wore a head scarf and a shawl. (Courtesy Curtright and Son Tribal Art.)

An unidentified gentleman and two women, one with her back to the camera, smoke clams on the beach around 1890. Images of Indians in the Pacific Northwest were sold by photographic firms that specialized in providing stereo views of the West to the millions who learned about the world through these three-dimensional images. Sometimes photographers asked permission and paid a fee; most times, as in this instance, they shot the picture they wanted. Although this image is unidentified, the seagoing canoe in the background suggests this picture might have been taken on Quinault homelands. (Courtesy Curtright and Son Tribal Arts.)

The Cushman Indian Hospital participated in the 1950 Daffodil Parade in Puyallup, Washington, with a float. The hospital closed in 1959, and it was not until 1974 that the Puyallup tribe secured funds to establish a medical clinic that treats all Indian people, including Nisquallys. Today the Takopid Medical Center serves over 30,000 people a year. (Courtesy Washington State Historical Society.)

Ben Hicks, a World War II veteran, poses in his living room around 1950. He was a descendant of Peter Kalama and his second wife. The Hicks family had land on the old reservation that now forms part of Fort Lewis. Ben's son is currently an Indian fish commissioner. (Courtesy Nisqually Indian Tribe Archive.)

In this c. 1900 formal portrait, Ruby Parsons Wells poses with her daughter Mary. (Courtesy Nisqually Indian Tribe Archive.)

Cushman Indian Hospital, located on the Puyallup Reservation, served Indians and Alaska natives as well as other patients. Pictured here on a visiting day in 1950, family members wait to

see their loved ones. Nisqually tribal members who live in Pierce County still go to Puyallup for health services. (Courtesy Washington State Historical Society.)

Lillian Iyall poses in front of her home while her nephew Art (in a sailor's cap) sits on the porch railing in the background, around 1940. Art is the father of Nisqually tribal chair Cynthia Iyall. (Courtesy Nisqually Indian Tribe Archive.)

Finley LeClair, age nine, was photographed around 1900. His descendants work on the Nisqually and Squaxin Reservations. (Courtesy Nisqually Indian Tribe Archive.)

Frank's Landing—where key events in fishing rights history took place—now has a convenience store with a parking lot.

Nisqually employees at the tribal office prepare for the 2006 canoe journey. The tribe provides employment in the casino, two fish hatcheries, and tribal government. (Courtesy Lou Ann Squally.)

Melvin Iyall (left) and Billy Frank (right) pose with and an unidentified friend on the old homestead on what is now Fort Lewis. Willie Frank, Billy's father, purchased six acres of bottomland on the west side of the river after being displaced. This spot became known as Frank's Landing, a key battle site in the fish wars of the 1960s and 1970s. (Courtesy Nisqually Indian Tribe Archive.)

An old Indian homestead can be seen in the distance in what is now Fort Lewis. This photograph was taken when the old reservation was condemned and Nisqually families lost their homes. Today the tribe actively buys land and restores properties they already own—dikes on the old Braget farm in Nisqually, for example, were leveled by the tribe to encourage survival of the salmon. (Courtesy Nisqually Indian Tribe Archive.)

122

Elders and youth meet at the blessing of the canoe with the ritual greeting, which involves the raising of hands. Raised hands are often seen on welcoming figures. (Courtesy Lou Ann Squally.)

Army-sponsored site visits to the old reservation on Fort Lewis provide elders with the opportunity to walk on ancestral lands. Army archaeologists work with elders to interpret the material culture, such as old glass shards found on the site. This evidence helps develop a biography of Nisqually land.

Camas covers Squally Plain on the Fort Lewis section of the old reservation. This picture was taken in May 2007 during a visit by Nisqually elders. It was sponsored by the army. The army and tribe work together on many projects of mutual benefit.

The Nisqually River Watershed remains the lifeline of the tribe. Investments of time and money by the tribe work to make the Nisqually the cleanest and wildest river in the country. The tribe supports the nonprofit Nisqually Land Trust, which purchases land from private property owners in order to maintain the health of the river. Muck Creek, pictured here in 2007, is home to one-third of the salmon in the watershed. Restoration efforts have made this miracle possible.

Nisqually youth continue the work of their elders. In 2006, drums and other traditional regalia were made on the reservation by youth as part of the canoe journey. (Courtesy Lou Ann Squally.)

Nisqually Lake waits silently on the Fort Lewis side of the old reservation. Perhaps one day this land will be returned to the Nisqually.

SUGGESTED READING

American Friends Service Committee. *Uncommon Controversy: Fishing Rights of Muckleshoot, Puyallup and Nisqually Indians*. Seattle: University of Washington Press, 1972.

Ballard, Arthur C. *Mythology of Southern Puget Sound*. Seattle: University of Washington Press, 1929.

Berkhofer, Robert F. Jr. *The White Man's Indian: Images of the American Indian from Columbus to the Present*. New York, Knopf, 1978.

Chaplin, Ralph. *Only the Drums Remembered*. Tacoma, WA: Tahoma Research Services, 1960.

Carpenter, Cecelia. *Fort Nisqually: A Documented History of Indian and British Intervention*. Tacoma, WA: Tahoma Research Services, 1986.

———. *Leschi: Last Chief of the Nisquallies*. Tacoma, WA: Tahoma Research Services, 1986.

———. *The Nisqually, My People*. Tacoma, WA: Tahoma Research Services, 2003.

———. *Tears of Internment, the Indian History of Fox Island and the Puget Sound Indian Wars*. Tacoma, WA: Tahoma Research Services, 1996.

Duwamish et al, vs. the United States of America, Consolidated Petition No. F-275. Seattle: Argus Press, 1993.

Haeberlin, Hermann and Erna Gunther. *The Indians of Puget Sound*. Seattle: University of Washington Press, 1930.

Heath, Joseph. *Memoirs of Nisqually*. Fairfield, WA: Ye Galleon Press, 1979.

Miller, Jay. *Lushootseed Culture and the Shamanic Odyssey: An Anchored Radiance*. Lincoln: University of Nebraska Press, 1999.

Pascaly, Maria and Cecelia Carpenter. *Remembering Medicine Creek: the Story of the First Treaty Signed in Washington*. Seattle: Fireweed Press, 2004.

Smith, Marian. *The Puyallup-Nisqually*. New York: Columbia University Press, 1940.

Trafzer, Clifford E., ed. *Indians, Superintendents, and Councils: Northwestern Indian Policy, 1850–1855*. Lanham, MD: University Press of America, 1986.

Visit us at
arcadiapublishing.com